Eigengrau

Eigengrau

Poems
2015 to 2020

Madison Scott-Clary

Also by Madison Scott-Clary

Arcana — A Tarot Anthology, ed.

Rum and Coke — Three Short Stories from a Furry Convention

Restless Town

All works © Madison Scott-Clary. These works are licensed under the Creative Commons Attribution 4.0 International License. To view a copy of this license, visit *creativecommons.org/licenses/by/4.0/* or send a letter to Creative Commons, PO Box 1866, Mountain View, CA 94042, USA.

This book uses the fonts Gentium Basic, Gentium Book Basic, and **Inknut Antiqua** and was typeset with X∃LATEX.

ISBN: 978-1-948743-14-3

Eigengrau

First Edition, 2019.

10 9 8 7 6 5 4 3 2 1

	Foreword	vii
1	Solitary works	1
2	Unimportant verse about important people	17
3	Poems from Missives	29
4	Mental Health	37
5	Gender	53
6	Collected haiku	67

Foreword

What is the color of a moonless night? Of closed eyes in a darkened room? Of the edge of sleep?

One might be tempted to say "black", but this is not so. In those lightless places on the edge of vision, strange biophysical effects take hold. After all, the mind and the eye would rather reserve purest black for contrast — that black is "that which is the darkest thing I can see".

But what do they do when everything is the same dim hue, when even those hue-sensitive cones have too little light to work with? In such a liminal state, even the occasional staticky hiccups of the rods' excitement look like color to an input-starved brain; in the absence of information, it over-interprets noise. This color is called Eigengrau, which we might calque as "own gray", or perhaps more poetically as "intrinsic gray" – that liminal shade that the mind turns to when all other color is lost to it.

This collection, then, is named after a liminal color, unknown to pigment and light; in some sense an impossible color. Such has been the pleasure of my experience these past five years with Madison. From the very earliest days that I have known her, I have felt something slightly slippery, something intense in some difficult-to-express way, about her presentation of herself. As I have taught her of Eigengrau, she has taught me of liminality, and I cannot help but feel that this wondrous exchange is a microcosm of our friendship. Who and what I would be, not having known her, beggars my imagination; certainly I would be impoverished by the lack.

And just as she has left her beneficial marks on me, so have many others left marks on her; scattered throughout these pages are crystalline memories in ink. They are fingerprints left in clay by acquaintances and lovers and absent friends and ideas and moods, little slices through reality preserved in glass. They are a quiet glimpse into carefully curated parts of her soul; should rescue simulations ever come to pass, I have no doubt that this book will form a crucial part of the reconstruction for hers, and thus perhaps for mine, for scattered among those glimmering memories I recognize fragments of myself.

Close, then, your eyes, and look upon the color you carry always with you, that lightless, liminal color barely known to art or to science. Gaze upon Eigengrau. Then open your eyes and gaze with delight upon *Eigengrau*.

— Lorxus

For Margaras

Solitary works

The dogs assure me

March, 2015

The dogs assure me:
There are volumes of meaning —
Life and death —
And time;
Past, present, future —
In the scent of a rotting fish left after the flood,
Or a trace of scat,
Or the coyote, long passed,
But not everyone reads poetry.

I'm not so lucky, all told:
The rich scent of meaning —
Heady, intoxicating —
Rises only from words
And the way you rest your hands on the table.

Published in <u>Civilized Beasts, 2016 Edition</u>.

A year starts not on January first

October, 2019

A year starts not on January first.
    The days may hunder but the seasons speak
of time's long march, of fast time, slow time. Thirst
    for "start" and "end" neglects the limen sleek.
So, why do some unsubtle sciences
    forget about the in-betweens? Those pure
uncolored dreams made mere contrivances;
    "between the years" now simply: "year, then year".
These rough mechanics, held unseen, can spoil
    the beauty of our silent spaces, take
from us the liminality, embroil
    our lives in cold and tired minutiae.
        Come sit with me, come stay with me inside
        this place between where strange new loves abide

★

"So, what does it mean?"

She shrugged and sipped her tea.

They sat together in silence for a while.

"There's something about the liminal that terrifies me."

        "Me too," she said...

Growth

July, 2018

Used to be you and I daily would walk
through the fields out back of the house and talk
for hours, spilling words and emotions.
These walks were our daily devotions
to each other over the years.

The fields, dotted with ponds, were our space.
We tramped those trails strung like lace
along shores and through tall grass,
murmuring now like winds, chattering now like brass
in some changeful duet.

You'd tell me about the geese in the sky,
would watch me stand still and not ask why
the birds scared me to pieces,
even as we dodged around their feces
littering the trails.

You'd put up with my fickle interests,
running with me, or stopping to see what arrests
my attention. You'd follow all of my changes
and change along with me through all the ranges
of our shared experience.

You'd tell me of your meditation,
I'd talk of my fears of stagnation.
You'd always smile so kindly to me,
and I'd always feel so free
in our companionship.

And over time, those walks got slower,
shorter, less frequent, or over
far too soon, though no less meaningful
as we spent our time together in cheerful
conversation or kind quiet.

We each seemed to be going our separate ways,
with me branching out, exploring different lays
of different lands, and you turning inwards,
exploring lines of thought you never put in words,
at least not that you told me.

And then one day, we once more went out walking
and though it took a while, you got to talking.
You told me of how you sat, quiet and alone,
waiting for the time you might turn to stone
and be completely still at last.

You told me how as you sat, the room lengthened,
curved around, turned on you — strengthened,
it seemed, by your very presence —
and amid all of that gathered pleasance,
bit you in half.

You told me how, as part of you died
in that moment, the rest of you spied,
it seemed, on this very ending.
You told me you thought that this rending
was the end of something big.

I listened in silence. What could I say?
The things you were telling me, walking that day
were strangely shaped and didn't make sense.
Or if they did, they did so around corners as pretense,
perhaps, subtext, allusion, metaphor.

You were right, though, I could hear it in your voice.
There was finality, there, which spoke of a choice
already made. Endings were writ on your face,
your hands, and your steps — your very pace
spoke of completion.

I replied to that sense rather than your words.
"While you look up to the geese and see only birds,
I see omens and my doom spelled in vees.
You speak of rooms and cleaving, but please,
tell me, are you leaving?"

We'd long since stopped, there by the pond,
and your smile was, yes, sad, but still fond
as you settled down wordlessly to your knees,
took a slow breath, looked out to the trees,
and closed your eyes.

Beginnings are such delicate times
and I very nearly missed it, no chimes
to announce the hour of your leaving.
As it was, there was no time for believing
or not in the next moments.

Your fingers crawled beneath the soil
and sprouted roots, flesh starting to roil.
Coarse bark spiraled up your wrists and arms,
Spelling subtle incantations and charms
to the chaos of growth.

You bowed your head and from your crown
sprouted a tender shoot covered in fine down,
soon followed by crenelated leaves and fine stems.
The pace was fast, implacable, and leaves like gems
soon arched skyward.

You sprouted and grew, taking root
in one smooth motion, fixed and mute.
Your clothing fell away, rotting in fast-time.
Naked now, you sat still, committing one last crime
of indecency.

Your face, your face! In your face was such peace
as I'd never seen, even as you gave up this lease
on life, echoed also in my heart of hearts.
I did not cry out, nor even speak, witnessing such arts
as your final display showed.

Soon, you were consumed, transformed as a whole.
Your head a crown of leaves, your heart a bole
bored in rough bark and sturdy wood,
your fingers, knees, and toes stood
as thirsty roots.

I stood a while by the tree that was you,
then sat at your roots and thought of all I knew
about time, transformation, death and change.
I thought about you, your life, your emotional range,
your gentle apotheosis.

Then I walked home, quiet and numb.
No, not numb, per se, but perhaps dumb.
Dumb of words, dumb of emotions. Quiet.
I expected turmoil, some internal riot,
I got nullity.

Who, after all, if I cried out,
would hear my wordless shout
among the still trees and rustling leaves?
Who hears? Who cares? Who perceives
this non-grief?

You, my friend, are still there.
I walk the fields every day, passing where
you changed into something new.
I marvel at you, at how you grew
into something wholly different.

Used to be you and I daily would walk
through the fields out back of the house and talk.
Now, it's just me, alone, quiet, thinking
of you by the shore, forever drinking
of sweet water.

When I fall, I will remain whole

November, 2016

I keep hoping that, one day,
I'll spring palladial from the bole of a tree.
Fully formed, asexual,
Conceived without desire or intent.

My body will be virgin and clean,
My mind fresh, my soul at ease.
The tree, behind me, will stand crooked,
Bole seeping until time and air dry sap.

I will be a flat expanse of green, made up of new cells.
Everything will work together, a machine running smoothly.

I keep hoping to, one day,
Function with unity, unflagging.
Organized and purposeful,
Intent only on fulfillment.

My vision will be clear and unclouded,
My will affirming, strong, and sure.
And when I fall, I will remain whole,
Confident that I lived well and unapologetic.

I know there's rest

October, 2019

The eighteenth whisker on the left is brown.
    I know this after countless nights awake
beside you, watching every quiet breath.
    You puff your whiskers out on every yawn.
On longer work-filled days, your whiskers wilt,
    exhaustion softening your features, sleep
exerting subtle gravities to lead
    you to oneiric seas and dreamlike sands.
I know this after countless nights awake.
    I know, I know, it's strange to watch you sleep,
but when I can't, to know that someone can...
    at least it somehow lets me rest in turn.
When I lay beside your sleeping form
    I know there's rest to still be had for me.

Every time I fall

August, 2017

Every time I fall,
    The ground tells me I'm in love.
"'Cause love is
    All low," it says.
"And loves is
    Places."

And I always argue,
    That love is all people.
That love is dogs,
    And cats.
And love is
    Emotions.

But every time I fall,
    The ground tells me I'm in love.
That gravity is
    Some awkward embrace,
And love is
    Permanence.

And I always argue,
    That love is temporary.
That that's
    The beauty,
And permanence
    Misses the point. And every time I fall,
    The ground tells me I'm in love.
And every single time,
    I keep coming back.

Meaning & Self

February, 2017

There's some duality between sources of meaning,
    Between the types of stories we use to back identity.
It's not quite good & bad or light & dark,
    Though I'm not yet sure just how to define it.

Dad used to punish the dogs
    by locking then in the basement.
If he was really mad,
    he'd toss then down there by the scruff.

Mom moved me & her dogs to a new house —
    moved us three days early during the divorce.
Her dog punched my ex stepdad in the crotch the night before,
    the nut-shot to end all nut-shots, & our time there.

Few things make me feel as deeply about life as parenthood,
    even if it's just me caring for my dogs.
Some reminders of that are intense enough to be raw, painful,
    salt in the wounds of mortality, maybe, or the ache of maternal
        love.

The meaning behind the story of me & my dogs
    comes with a story of its own, or maybe several.
It's bound up in stories to come,
    & these stories nest infinitely deep.

Remembering that & shaping that,
    It's a part of making the meaning in my life.
This isn't better against worse,
    it's not mom against dad.

It's not a dichotomy at all, really,
    now that I think about it.
It's something subtler, comfortably complex, a topic of its own.
    I guess it's just meaning & self.

Unimportant verse about important people

—

February, 2017

I see your past in cross-processed film,
in blown-out colors and over-saturation.
    You told me all about it, told me grand stories:
    you were going to go back in time and save the world.
I see your past in yellows and browns,
in umber and sienna and amber, in a younger sun.
    You sat and told me how — and you were always sitting —
    you thought past-you dreamt of a future less complicated than
        today.
I see your past through film-grain and vignette,
with a thick white border, space on the bottom to write.
    You told me how you learned so many imperfect things,
    in so many less than ideal ways, always at inopportune times.
I see your past in architectural drawings of unrealized buildings,
in paperback covers reaching towards heaven, in trillions of words.
    You figured past you dreamt of, not perfection,
    but a world unconstrained by so many failures.
I see your past with no me in it,
and wonder if past-you dreamt of us.

—

February, 2017

Resuscitating ancient coins in class, we learned,
takes a toothbrush and olive oil.
Slow, steady strokes across, around...
soft bristles dislodging soil
one speck at a time.
But no one that day was nearly as blessed,
seeing a coin shine through
at the end, full relief brightly expressed,
as I was to see you smile.

—

February, 2017

When you arrive,
the whole world gets slow.
Sluggish, amber-colored air
mellows lively conversations.
Everyone stops, marvels,
turns eagerly toward you;
and there are no complaints
about warming our faces in the sun.

February, 2017

We fit together in the strangest ways
and seem to seek new seams to savor.
Such joins are hardly perfect,
thread tugging fabric unevenly
unless it's reinforced over and over again.
We seem to seek new seams to savor,
and, weak though they are,
revel in the imperfect unevenness of joining.

—

February, 2017

Complementary, clashing anxieties.
Dull clamor of intersecting feelings.
Need, desire, craving, jealousy.
Worry, fear, care, prayerful fretting.
Love, lust, friendship, a need to share.
Emotions on emotions on emotions,
and, often, comfortable silence.

—
May, 2017

Tightly wound springs
Of very carefully
Not touching.
    Secret words
    To be said
    With confidence.
Rules.
Prohibitions.
Limits.
    Discussions planned,
    Side-channels arranged,
    Whiskey purchased.
And now anxiety
Over what it means
And how to work it.
    Is it worth it for
    Long-standing questions
    To be answered?
To invite disaster
For sake of knowledge
And further dreams?
    Maybe the answer
    Is that tired refrain:
    Perhaps, perhaps, perhaps.
And now we're
Awaiting weeks
Of careful touches.

—

August, 2017

I could never tell you
that you feel too much.
That you feel too hard,
or that your feelings
overwhelm and overtake you.

I could never tell you
how beautiful that is.
That I wish I could feel those things,
that I wish I could feel that way.

All I can tell you
is how beautiful you are
when you feel love.

August, 2017

Yit'gadal v'yit'kadash sh'mei raba
Would that I had the faith
To pray daily.
Eleven months to let you go,
And an amen to end the sorrow.

—

June, 2018

Between our houses,
there is a simple fence -
not a chasm, not a wall.
Chain-link, waist high,
bedecked with sweet-pea
and set about with violets.
Something we can tend,
something to feel good about,
something between us
other than nothing.

—

May, 2019

I will swallow my love for you.
I will swallow my love.
I will swallow my love for you
And relish the magnesium flare,
Rejoice in immolation,
Cherish the autolysis
Of secret cells.
I will swallow my love for you.
I will swallow my love.

Poems from Missives

Though the flow'r may bloom ere long

February, 2017

Though the flow'r may bloom ere long
    and night recede unto the dawn,
so yet may love's embrace grow fond
    and still be spoilt upon the wan.
Brave are you and wield your smile:
    A cudgel, tool, a keen-edged blade.
You are not wan, love is not spoilt;
    thus I be slain and love not fade.
Have I any need for flow'rs?
    For nights, for dawns, for words or breath?
With so keen and fond a blade,
    There's naught to fear in life or death.
        So slay, then slay! For now, I care not how,
        I need for naught but that which love allow.

Delay, then, the morn

February, 2017

Though every climax approach a denouement
And every dawn a night,
Every moment worth sharing
May be worth stealing.
    Were it with you,
    Delay, then, the morn.

When every touch lingers as if forever
And yet seems to pass too soon,
Hearts reach out to hearts,
To seek, to aim, to keep.
    Were it with you,
    Delay, then, the morn.

Surely it's cruelty that need begets need begets need,
And yet need may bring pleasure.
Pleasure may hurt, ache, burn,
May steal hours of night.
    Were it with you,
    Delay, then, the morn.

Thy gift

February, 2017

I reach for the ewer of water,
I hope to quench the heat.
I beg for yet another serving,
I hope to fill my need.

The water — cool — cools not
Without thy merry presence.
The food fills, passes, is gone —
Yet leaves me empty, yearning.

Though the heart may quicken —
Though the tongue may lap —
I shall sup no greater meal
Than thy gift entrancing.

You find me at a disadvantage

February, 2017

On reading letters late received,
I felt within: the fox —
Yelping, yowling now, crying needfully —
Myself, a craving beast.

You find me at a disadvantage —
Panting and aswish —
Would that distance be traversed as easily
As hearts t'wards yearning hearts!

A rose, single, now blooming

February, 2017

A rose, single, now blooming
    may indeed bless the stem,
yet are not roses clipp'd and shown?
    Undoubted 'tis a blessing to them
who receive such a gift!
    Yet now unmade is the flow'r
which adorns thy mantle with its grace
    and withers, however slowly, by the hour,
        until 'tis faded to nothing and dust,
            though some scent remain forever amidst the must.

A rose, single, now blooming
    is perhaps best left on the stem,
its beauty to be admired amidst the growth.
    Surely 'tis better to long for that gem,
than witness beauty wilt and dry!
    Yet now one must long indeed, must burn,
Must yearn forever for that grace.
    To watch that growth, to explore stem's turn,
        day by day would destroy, weakening one by the hour,
            A rose, single, now blooming, forever holds all pow'r.

Mental Health

There is too much fire in me

                                                                June, 2016

There is too much fire in me
to be described by the soldering iron's tip.

If I were to draw that across my flesh,
    it would all spill out at once.
I'd melt, eaten whole by flames,
    and flow into a pool of molten silver.
I would be borne up through the clouds,
    and grow lighter by the second.
Sublimation would claim me then,
    atoms would scatter, diffuse.
All that energy poured to the air around me,
    an imperceptible increase in temperature.
Particle would excite particle
    until I'm felt only as warmth on your face.

But even that would not be enough.

Heligoland

February, 2017

Too many wine-dark seas need daily traversal,
And here the shipping forecast calls for rain.

The shipping forecast! What a load of bollocks.
You can listen from start to finish
And not hear a single word about how a day will feel.

Or maybe it's a pale, tired, steganography:
Moderate, becoming poor, violent storm 11.

Burning up, drowning, torn by wind, and all I can manage
is to tell you southwest gale 8 to storm 10.

I can point at the moon, exhausted, bored, decaying,
And hope you don't stare blankly at my finger.

Thanks to Lorxus

Bruise Vision

June, 2017

I

Geese Level:	A hundred geese overhead —
Unnerving	A thousand —
Expect:	A million —
anxiety	

Heady scent of premonition.
Acrid tang of ill omens.
Portents.
Too much meaning
    In too small a space.

II

Geese Level:	Geese are a byproduct of laminar shear
Noise-Cancelling	stress
Headphones	Of two layers of phantasmagorical
Expect:	Newtonian fluids,
auditory	Which is why they're often seen on
aberrations	a plane.
	A thin, sort-of Truth
	From a sort of thin layer
	geese chromatography.

III

Geese Level: As the dove bears the olive branch,
Eldrich   so too the goose bears the wand
Expect: that withers all it touches.
red tint to   A wand of nightshade,
vision; hot   Core of tainted silver.
flashes   A wand of obscure origin,
                 The goose surely stole it.
              Malice begets malice.

IV

Geese Level: We know not the transgression,
Beyond   the origin —
Comprehension   We know not the punishment,
Expect: only the terror.
confusion;
nausea;
sweating; racing
pulse

V

Geese Level:	Geas
Excruciating	Wing
Expect:	Dark
pounding heart;	Horizon
tunnel vision;	
racing thoughts;	
black outs; blood	
pouring from	
ears	

VI

Geese Level: I'd rather owls.
Terrifying   Owls, as though geese were turned
Expect: inside out,
tinnitus;   made less evil.
piloerection;   Still portentous,
shortness of   Still momentous,
breath; uneven   Just less terrifying.
gait

VII

      Geese Level: Life within a comfortable grid.
    Uncomfortable   Parallel lines
          Expect: Interrupting narrowing circles
        subdermal   Of birds in flight.
           itching;   Travel in straight lines.
        formication   Turn at right angles.
                             Trace the roof of your mouth
                                  With wet tongue.

VIII

Geese Level: Ritual thinking
       Birds   Driven by geese —
    Expect: By lines, by grids, by food —
       birds   By numbers and neat delineation.
                   And I'm left with questions:
                         Why the portents?
                         Why the anxiety?
                   Or maybe:
                         Did I take my meds this morning?

                   Failing that,
                         Can I just have the comfort of prayer
                         Or the ecstasy of signs
                               Without bleak paranoia
                               Over circling birds?

Beneath her coat was a whole identity

January, 2018

Beneath her coat was a whole identity:
A subtle form of ideas under soft fur,
A constantly shifting mass of meaning...
And somehow, she pulled it off.

She would go for days without shedding a thing,
And then, as if a bottle rolling off a counter,
She would shatter, sending shards of self flying,
And then we'd all see.

Then we'd all see the terror, the joy,
Then we'd all see the grief at nothing,
Then we'd all hear her say,
"I'm not built for a life with death in it."

And slowly, she'd pick herself back up
And find a brand new way to piece herself together
And build herself a brand new smile
And brush out her coat once more.

First-place winner of the Typewriter Emergencies Poetry contest.

Asertu

September, 2018

Disvolvu mian haŭton el mia karno.
Verŝu mian sangon el mi kiel vino.
Prenu mian vivon, tenu ĝin sub via lango:
   Amara pilolo por gustumi.

Bruligu min, entombigu min poste.
Loku ŝtonon super kie mi kuŝas.
Lasu tempo manĝi vian memorojn pri mi:
   Lasta peceto por gustumi.

★

Unwind my skin from my flesh.
Pour my blood from me like wine.
Take my life, hold it beneath your tongue:
   A bitter pill to savor.

Burn me, then entomb me.
Place a stone over where I lie.
Let time eat your memories of me:
   A final morsel to savor.

Numeno

September, 2018

Inter ĝuo kaj timo
Estas loko de tro da signifo.
Apud kompreno, ekster saĝo,
Tamen ĝi tutampleksas.
Mi kompareble malgrandas
Kaj ĝi tro granda estas.
Nekomprenebla
Nekontestebla,
Senmova kaj ĉiam ŝanĝiĝema.

★

Between joy and fear
Is a place of too much meaning.
Next to understanding, outside wisdom,
It nonetheless expands.
I'm so small beside it
and it is too big.
Incomprehensible,
Incontestible,
Unmoving and always changing.

Rush

June, 2019

A flash of coppery sweetness,
A clearing of the sinuses,
A burst of unnamed colors,
A rush of creativity, of wonder,
Velvety softness, a low hum,
And then the wave recedes.

Gender

Somehow, she's me

                                                          April, 2018

Her hair is tied with a ribbon
    Saying "This is not for you."
She wears a pendant of stamped brass
    Saying "Non sum qualis eram."
"I have been a hero since birth,"
    She tells herself,
        As though that will somehow
            Explain her scars.

She pierced her own ears,
    But did a shit job of it.
Her tattoos tease around
    the edges of her identity.
Her bones are ley-lines,
    She tells herself,
        Strung with symbols
            Heady with meaning.

She has a certain "fuck you" inflected
    "Je ne sais quoi" about her.
Her clothes bespeak
    carefully constructed laziness.
"I've got my own style,"
    She tells herself,
        While doing all she can
            To not be seen.

She studied order through science
    and found it chaotic.
She studied chaos through music
    and found it inviable.
"I'll work with words."
    She tells herself
        She'll write a book,
            Or publish stories.

She wanted to be a bus driver
    when she grew up.
Then a linguist, then a biologist,
    Then a composer, a conductor.
She never wanted to be
    What she became;
        The irony of which
            Is not lost on her.

Post-op images

May, 2018

—

Saturday is for mechanics.
Sunday is for terror.
Monday is for acceptance.
Tuesday is for purging.
Wednesday is for anxiety.
Thursday is for sleep.

—

When I am asleep,
The world changes around me.
In spring, I am changed.

—

I'm no good at images, only words,
and yet for days after surgery,
as anesthesia and countless
    milligrams, milliliters, millions of
drugs leave my system,
I'm lousy with visions,
each lousy with meaning.

I lay in bed, unable to move,
struggling to keep my eyes open;
I know that if I close them,
    I'll be lost, I'll be lost, I'll be
mired in waking dreams,
coherent visions with all the logic
of that paler side of consciousness.

Perhaps the veil here
is still too thin and vague,
the pool too clear, the monsters too scary
    too lean, too mean, too hungry, or
perhaps I was too close to death
to come away totally unscathed,
too close to completely survive.

It's as though, laying here,
stinking of hospital,
I'm seeing emotions play out,
    Scene after scene, scene after scene,
anxiety shown in heaps of discarded entrails,
hope in the ceaseless ratcheting of gears,
determination in the marching of feet.

If I were an artist, perhaps
I could hope to touch these images,
but as it is, every word falls short,
    too vague, too inexact, too tight to
hope to explain something so vast
by the very act of attempting to reproduce;
I can only hint from the margins.

That poetry can accomplish what prose cannot
in its economy of motion
is attractive to me, here in recovery —
    so tired, so tired, so tired — so
maybe I can hope to express the dire import
of these visions dancing behind closed lids,
or at least remind myself on rereading.

Even now, a week out,
I'm starting to lose touch with the visions,
I can almost touch them if I squint,
    lie real still, don't move now, but
even then, a shadow of the substance...
I'm starting to consign to memory
that which was probably memory to begin with.

—

It is two hundred miles between what I expect and what I want.
Two hundred long strides that seem impossible from one direction,
    and from the other a day's short drive.

It is nine and a half hours between question and answer.
A half hour of jazz, nine hours of sleep, a scant second of perspective,
    and I can only traverse in one direction

It is eleven inches between who I was and who I am.
Ten of those inches are pain, the eleventh is numb,
    There's pleasure to be had in there, I'm promised.

It is twelve years between what I want and what I get:
Ten years of remembering who I will become, two years running,
    Eight days dreaming.

—

What have you changed?
> *My mind*

What changed you?
> *Nothing*

What became of it?
> *I am not who I was*

What have you changed?
> *My name*

What changed you?
> *The word*

What became of it?
> *I am called who I am*

What have you changed?
> *My looks*

What changed you?
> *The light*

What became of it?
> *I am seen as I am*

What have you changed?
> *My chemistry*

What changed you?
> *The substance*

What became of it?
> *My form is my own*

What have you changed?
> *My body*

What changed you?
> *The knife*

What became of it?
> *I am shaped how I am*

What have you changed?
> *Nothing*

What changed you?
> *I was accepted*

What became of it?
> *I accepted myself*

What have you changed?
> *Everything*

What changed you?
> *Everything*

What became of it?
> *I became who I am*

Fair and square

> July, 2018

I bought my name fair and square;
Bespoke, built from whole cloth.
I wrote it again and again,
Savoring every J,
Skipping every fifth tittle,
Until it felt right,
Like sitting inside and watching the snow fall
    Through the window
Or finding the perfect way that branches in two trees
    Line up with each other
Or when the windshield wipers move
    In time with your music.

I built myself fair and square
With hands raw from coarse identity.
I kneaded and pressed and squeezed,
Savoring every curve,
Skipping every tenth day,
Until it all felt right,
Like the sweet smell of pine bark
    Rubbed between fingers
Or the whisper of maple leaves
    Under hurrying paws
Or the perfect overlap of new buds
    Already sticky with sap.

Collected haiku

A measure of grain
and a measure of water —
spring's own time and heat

Air carries the scent
of myriads of lives spent
on summer's warm breath

Crumb and density,
warmth buried beneath crisp crust —
autumn's crackling leaves.

Loves and loaves and loaves
baked for comfort in the cold —
winter calls for stores.

Leaves fall, grass withers,
and I step back to witness
winter's frozen form.

Half an hour's silence,
body relaxing slowly,
letting springtime in.

A season to stretch,
then one to learn everything —
summer's exploring.

What will autumn bring?
Maturity? Strength? Wisdom?
Dry heat and cool nights?

Seven flies circle,
Trimmers chatter down the block:
The hum of summer.

    I listen, silent, waiting,
    Breathing in sun and out shade.

Fig leaves like fingers
paw feebly through still hot air
and come up with naught.

    Too early for fruit to droop,
    we must wait past midsummer.

And I walk until
all I can hear is the wind
among the fir trees.

    Summer breezes bear away
    all the choices of years past.

Drink deep of death-thoughts
as the day dies with a yawn —
the year starts to fade.

Arctic fox's den,
adorned with flowers and snow:
garden in winter.

www.ingramcontent.com/pod-product-compliance
Lightning Source LLC
Chambersburg PA
CBHW050332120526
44592CB00014B/2158